The World of Butterflies!

ACTIVITY BOOK FOR KIDS

MW01533737

Copyright © 2024 by SunnyLifeStudios™, a registered trademark of Virgo Media Group LLC.

All photography used is under the copyright of Alamy and iStock.

All rights reserved. No part of this book may be reproduced in any form or by any means, electronic, mechanical, photocopying or otherwise, without the written permission of the publisher.

All brand names and product names used in this book are trademarks, registered trademarks, or trade names of their respective holders. SunnyLifeStudios™ is not associated with any product or vendor in this book.

Acknowledgements: A heartfelt thank you to Jono Francis of *Douglas and Francis Safaris* of Zimbabwe for generously sharing his stunning butterfly photographs and expert knowledge. His firsthand experience offers a unique glimpse into the world of butterflies. To learn more or embark on your own wildlife adventure, visit *dfsafaris.com*.

Hello and Welcome to
The World of Butterflies!

Contents

About Butterflies

Welcome to the little book about The (BIG) World of Butterflies!

Did you know that butterflies have been fluttering around for more than 60 million years? There are over 18,000 species of these colorful creatures around the world!

Butterflies do more than just look pretty—they're super important to nature and our **ecosystem**.

Butterflies are **pollinators** that help plants grow by carrying pollen and are a key part of the food chain, providing meals for birds and other animals.

Even cooler, butterflies can sense changes in the environment faster than humans! This makes them tiny superheroes of nature, letting us know when something's wrong with their habitats.

Sadly, many butterfly species are in danger because their homes are being destroyed by pollution, deforestation, and climate change. But don't worry, you can work with **conservationists** to help protect them!

Check out some of the ideas of how you can take action to help the butterflies, on the following page!

In this book, you'll meet **eight beautiful butterflies** from around the world. Each one has a unique shape, color, and home!

As you color the pages and experiment with different shades, you'll discover fun facts about these beautiful creatures. Plus, with space for field notes, you can document your own butterfly sightings, and **turn this book into your very own butterfly adventure!**

Fun Butterfly Facts!

- **Butterfly** wings are transparent - the colors come from tiny scales!

- **Butterflies** taste with their feet - they can taste the leaves they land on!

- **Butterflies** don't fly at night or when it's too cold.

- While **butterflies** can't see far, they can spot ultraviolet colors we can't!

- Some **butterflies** even hire ants to protect their baby caterpillars by offering a sweet treat called honeydew.

How to Help Butterflies !

Plant a Butterfly Garden: Grow flowers that butterflies love, like milkweed, lavender, or daisies. You can make your backyard or balcony a butterfly-friendly space!

Create a "Butterfly Zone": Leave part of your yard or garden wild! Butterflies love messy areas with native plants where they can find food and shelter.

Build a Butterfly Bath: Butterflies need water too! Create a safe area for them to rest and drink by placing a shallow dish of water with pebbles in your garden.

Be a Butterfly Advocate: Share what you learn about butterflies with friends and family. The more people know, the more they'll want to help protect butterflies too!

Help Reduce Pollution: Remind your family to recycle, use less plastic, and keep nature clean to protect butterflies' homes.

Keep Exploring: Discover more about your favorite butterfly—where do they live, and what flowers do they love?

6

Color Theory
How to Create Butterflies Colors!

Color Theory

Color Wheel: Imagine a rainbow in a circle! Colors start darker at the edges and get lighter as they move to the center - like a sunset blending into a bright sky when you add white.

Primary Colors: Red, **Yellow**, and **Blue** are the building blocks of color! They're the starting point for creating all other colors.

Secondary Colors: Colors such as **Orange**, **Green**, and **Purple** are created by combining two primary colors. Most butterflies are a blend of different colors.

● = ● + ●   *Monarch*

● = ● + ●   *Emerald Swallowtail*

● = ● + ●   *Great Purple Emperor*

Tertiary Colors: These are the cool colors made when a primary color and a secondary color combine. The ***Queen Alexandra's Birdwing*** has wings of of **Blue Green** and **Yellow Green**!

Complementary Colors: Opposites attract!
Colors like **Red** and **Green**, or **Purple** and **Yellow**, sit across from each other on the color wheel. When they are side by side, they make each other stand out even more. Imagine the beauty of the ***Blue Morpho*** butterfly landing on an orange flower!

Color Theory

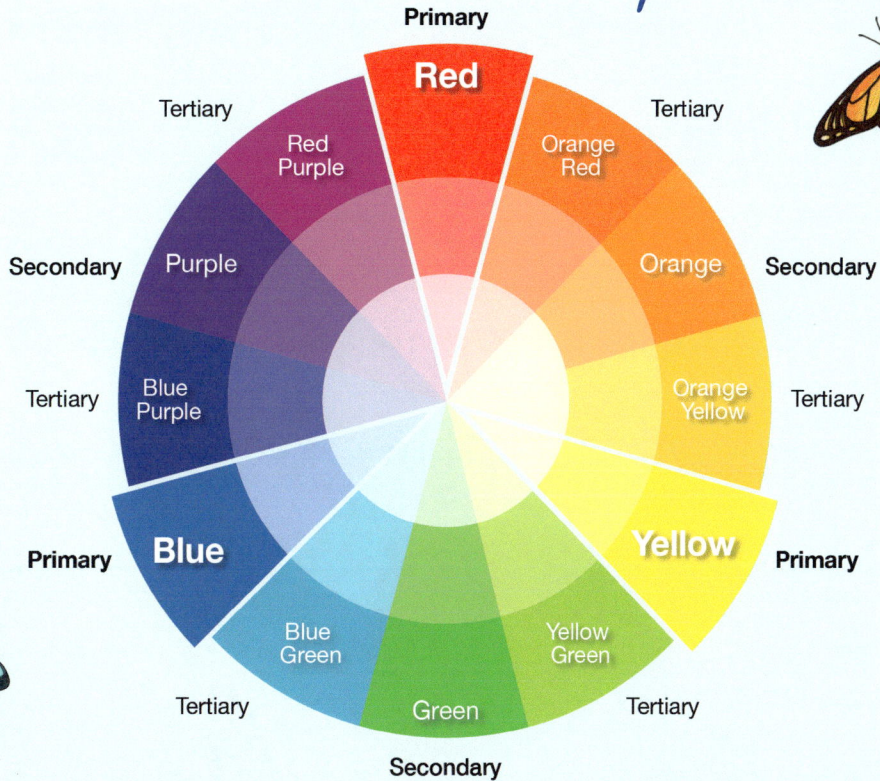

Primary

Red

Tertiary — Red Purple

Secondary — Purple

Tertiary — Blue Purple

Primary — **Blue**

Tertiary — Blue Green

Secondary — Green

Tertiary — Yellow Green

Primary — **Yellow**

Tertiary — Orange Yellow

Secondary — Orange

Tertiary — Orange Red

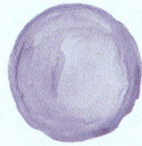

Orange

Purple

Pink

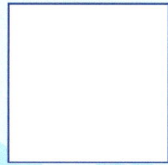
Dark Green

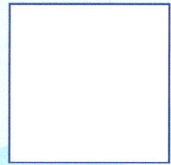
Light Blue

Mix colors (Red, Yellow, Blue, Black, White) to create the colors above! 9

Now it's Time to Meet
The Butterflies!

Color the butterflies!
use the following pages as
color guides. OR - use your
imagination to create
fantasy butterflies!

Queen Alexandra's Birdwing
(Ornithoptera alexandrae)

Location: Papua New Guinea

Habitat: Lowland tropical rainforest

Type: Swallowtail (Papilionidae)

Wingspan: Up to 11 inches (28 cm)!

Color: Males are bright gold, turquoise, blue and black. Females are brown and black, with white spots and triangles. Both have striking yellow abdomens!

Fun Fact: This butterfly was named after Queen Alexandra of Denmark, wife of King Edward VII. This butterfly's royal name reflects it's incredible size and beauty!

Can you imagine a butterfly with a wingspan as long as a ruler?

Blue Morpho
(Morpho peleides)

Location: South & Central America, parts of North America

Habitat: Rainforest

Type: Brush-footed (Nymphalidae)

Wingspan: 5.0-8.0 inches (13-20 cm)

Color: Males have shimmering blue upper wings edged with black. The bottom wings are a dull brown color, providing camouflage, or **crypsis**, against predators. Female morphos are usually brown or yellow.

Fun Fact: When it flies, the Blue Morpho's wings appear to flash blue and brown, making it hard for predators to track!

Monarch
(Danaus plexippus)

Location: North America, South & Central America, Australia, some Pacific Islands, Africa, Europe

Habitat: Grasslands, gardens

Type: Brush-footed (Nymphalidae)

Wingspan: 3.5-4.0 inches (9.0-10.2 cm)

Color: Vivid orange with black veins, edged with a black border speckled with white spots.

Fun Fact: Monarchs migrate over 3,000 miles to warmer places called **overwintering** grounds - some even travel all the way to Mexico!

Emerald Swallowtail
(Papilio palinurus)

Location: Southeast Asia (Indonesia, Thailand, Philippines, Malaysia)

Habitat: Tropical rainforests

Type: Swallowtail (Papilionidae)

Wingspan: 3.1-3.9 inches (7.9-9.9 cm)

Color: The upper wings are covered by powdery green scales on a background of dark green, with shiny emerald green metallic bands. The bottom wings are dark brown and orange.

Fun Fact: The green color on the Emerald Swallowtail's wings isn't from pigment, but from tiny scales that reflect light to create the color. This phenomenon is called **iridescence**!

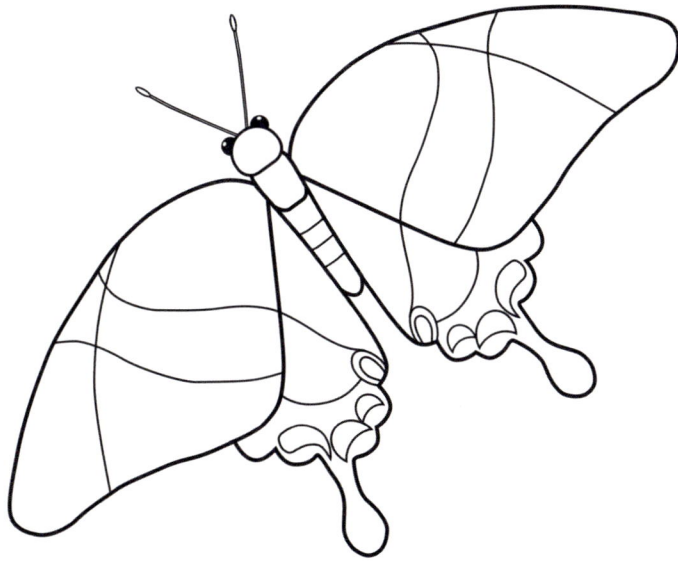
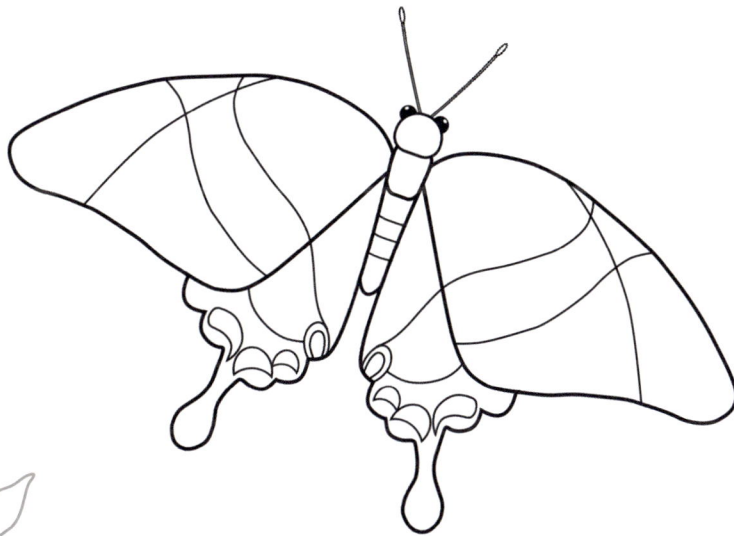

Great Purple Emperor
(Sasakia charonda)

Location: East Asia (Japan, Korea, China)

Habitat: Forests, woodlands

Type: Brush-footed (Nymphalidae)

Wingspan: 2.0-4.0 inches (5.1-10.2 cm)

Color: The upper wings of the males show a striking iridescent blue-purple color, bordered by brown dotted with yellow spots and a prominent red spot on the hindwings. The female butterflies have similar markings, but are mostly brown.

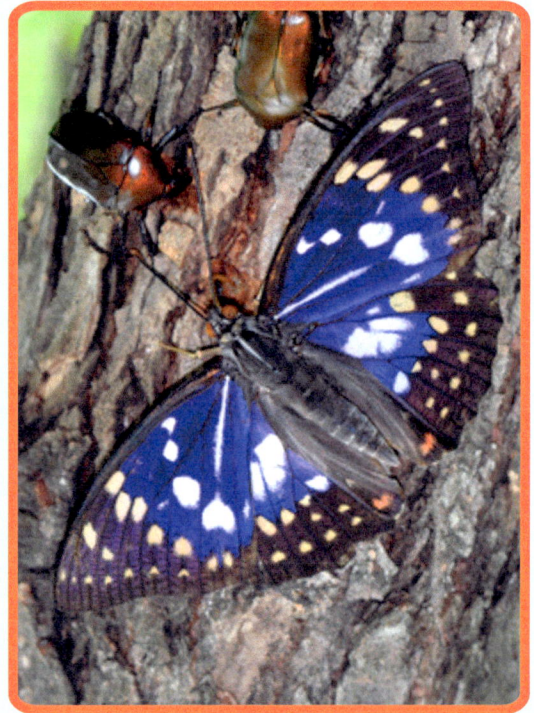

Fun Fact: The Great Purple Emperor is the national butterfly of Japan, where it is called "Oh-Murasaki". It is regarded as a symbol of resilience and good luck!

Purple-shot Copper
(Lycaena alciphron)

Location: Europe, North Africa, and across temperate Asia to Northern China

Habitat: Flowering meadows and grasslands. mountains

Type: Gossamer-winged (Lycaenidae)

Wingspan: 1.4-2.0 inches (3.6-5.1 cm)

Color: The upper wings of the males are bright orange with purple spots or streaks, while the females are brown with orange markings.

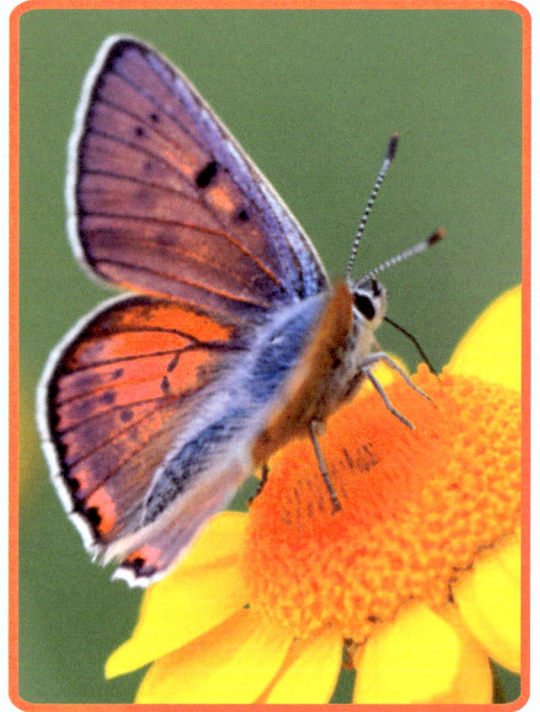

Fun Fact: The Purple-shot Copper males' wings shimmer with a purple tint that changes in sunlight, which helps attract females!

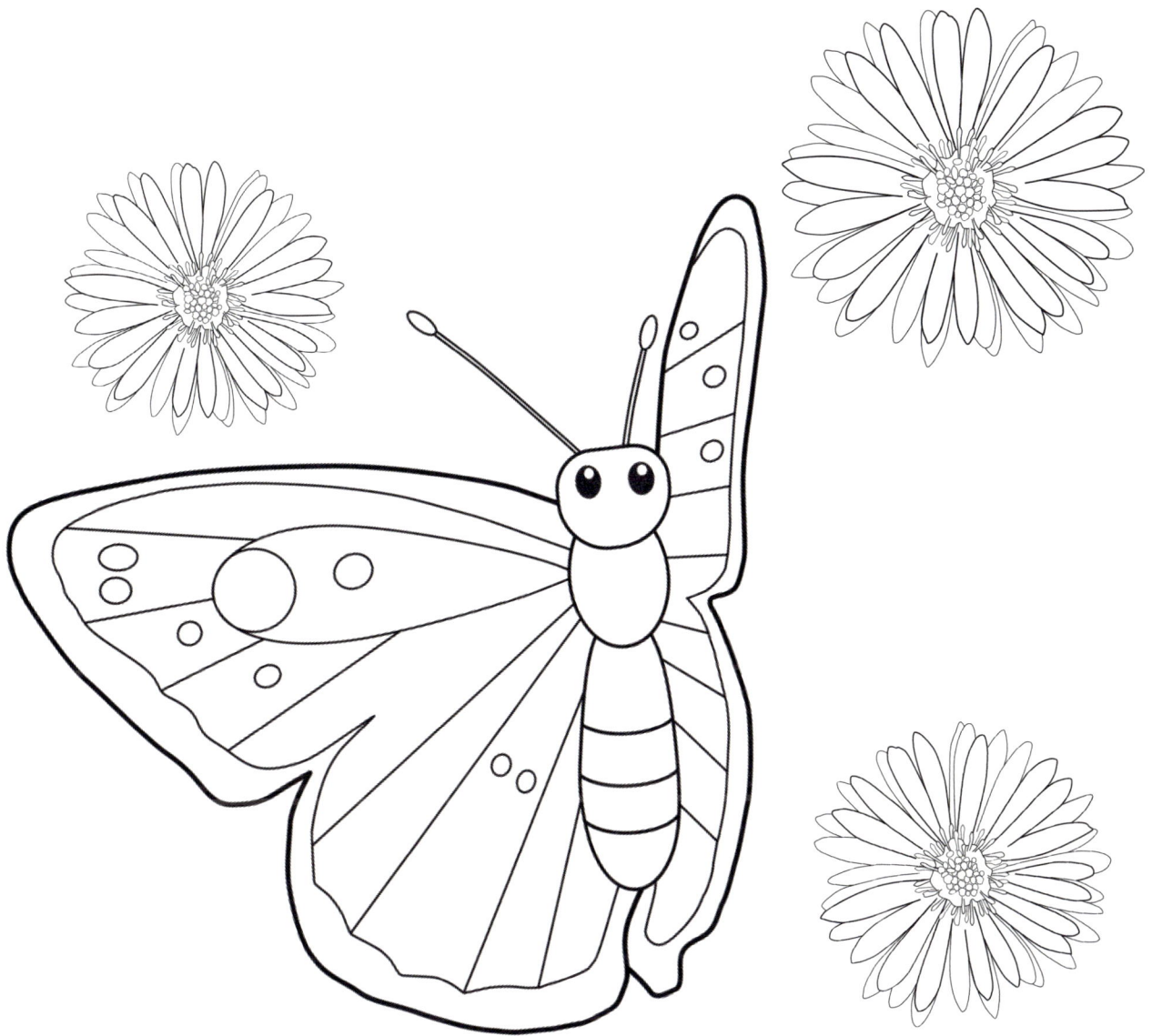

Blushing Phantom
(Cithaerias pireta)

Location: Central and South America, Africa

Habitat: Moist, shaded habitats, lowland rain forests

Type: Brush-footed (Nymphalidae)

Wingspan: 1.4-2.5 inches (3.5-6.4 cm)

Color: The wings of this butterfly are almost completely transparent, with hot pink blush-like markings on each hindwing.

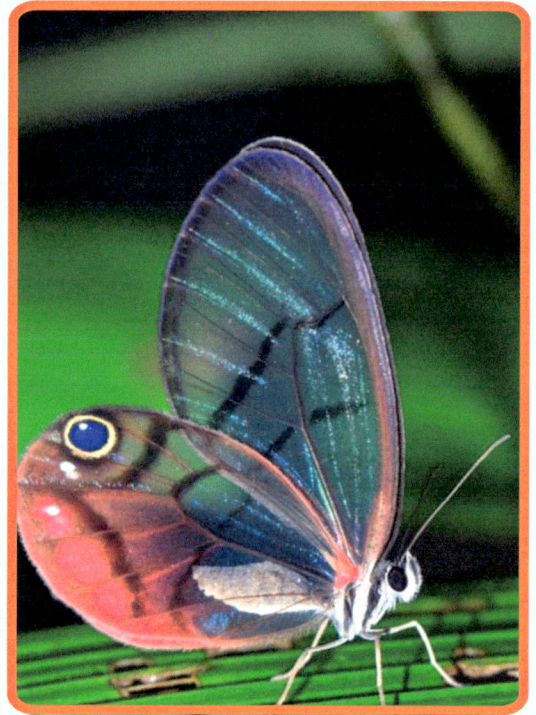

Fun Fact: The Blushing Phantom's transparent wings help it stay hidden from predators, blending into its surroundings.

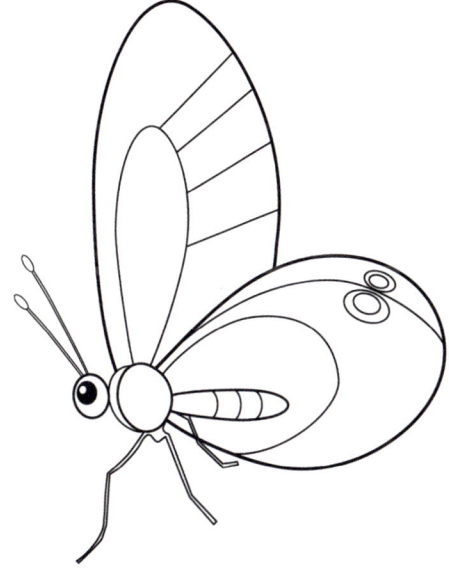

Lalos Sapphire
(Iolaus lalos)

Location: Moist, shaded habitats, lowland rain forests

Habitat: Forests and savannas

Type: Gossamer-winged (Lycaenidae)

Wingspan: 1.5 inches (3.8 cm)

Color: Vibrant sapphire blue color, with hindwings tipped in orange and pink.

Fun Fact: The Sapphire butterfly caterpillars mimic what they eat. Below is an example of a Sapphire butterfly larva mimicking a leaf, an excellent example of crypsis.

Look closely - do you see me?

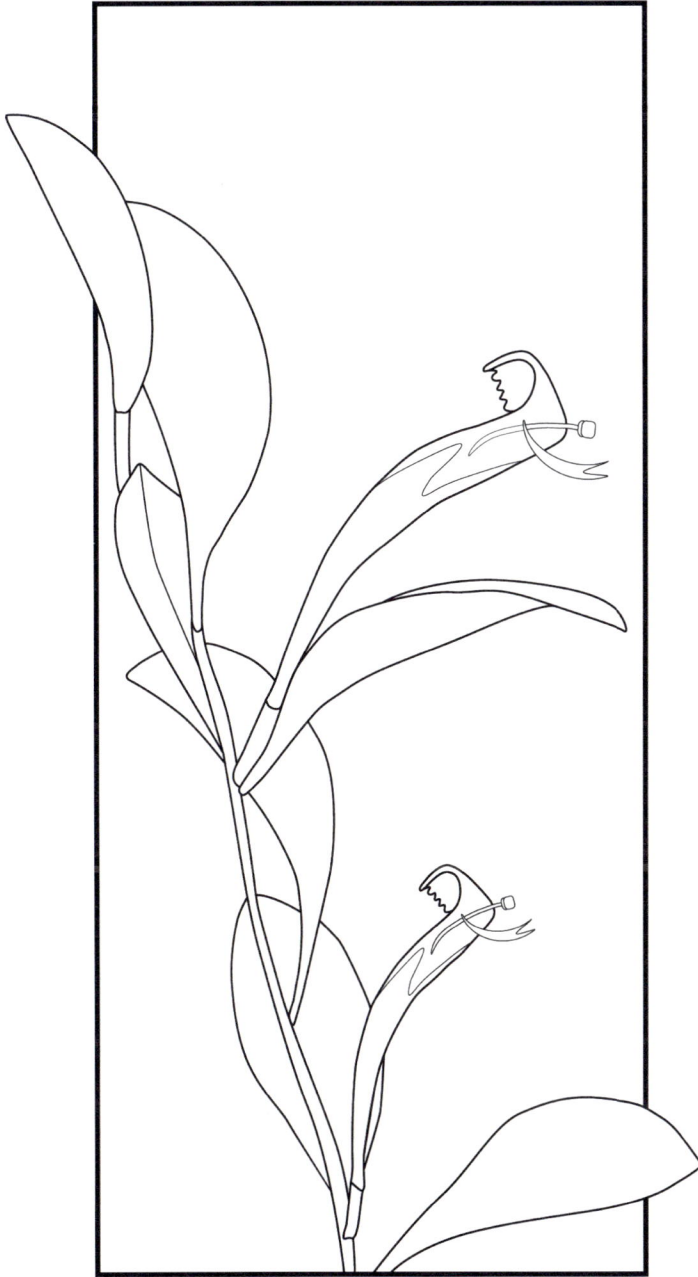
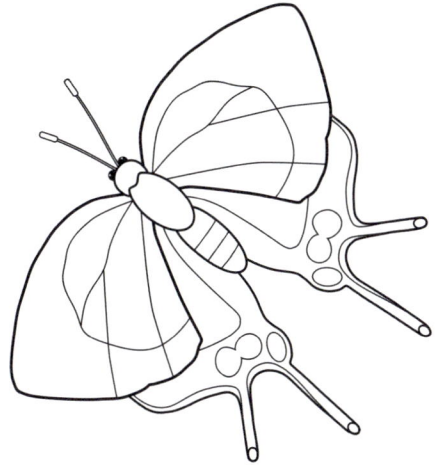
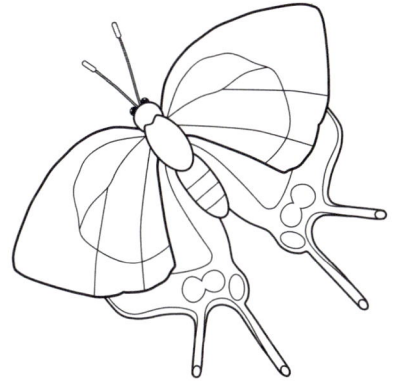
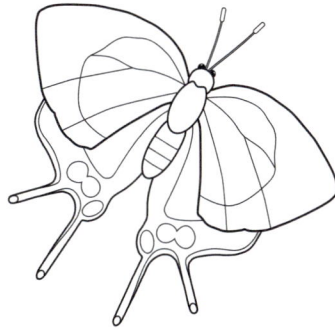

Butterfly Lifecycle

Metamorphosis: The amazing process where a butterfly transforms through four different stages in its life. Each stage looks completely different!

Eggs: A female butterfly looks for the perfect place to lay her eggs—usually on a **host plant** that her baby caterpillars will love to eat! The eggs keep the growing embryo safe until it's time to hatch.

Caterpillar: A tiny, hungry caterpillar hatches from its egg and starts munching away with its strong jaws, called **mandibles**. Some caterpillars grow to be 100 times bigger than when they were born!

Chrysalis: After lots of eating and growing, the caterpillar wraps itself in a protective case called a **chrysalis**. Inside, something incredible happens: the caterpillar's body breaks down and reforms into wings, legs, and other parts that will make it a butterfly!

Butterfly: Finally, the adult butterfly emerges from its chrysalis, ready to spread its wings and fly! Butterflies have four delicate wings covered with tiny, colorful scales. Unlike caterpillars, butterflies don't eat—they drink liquids using their long, straw-like mouthpart called a **proboscis**.

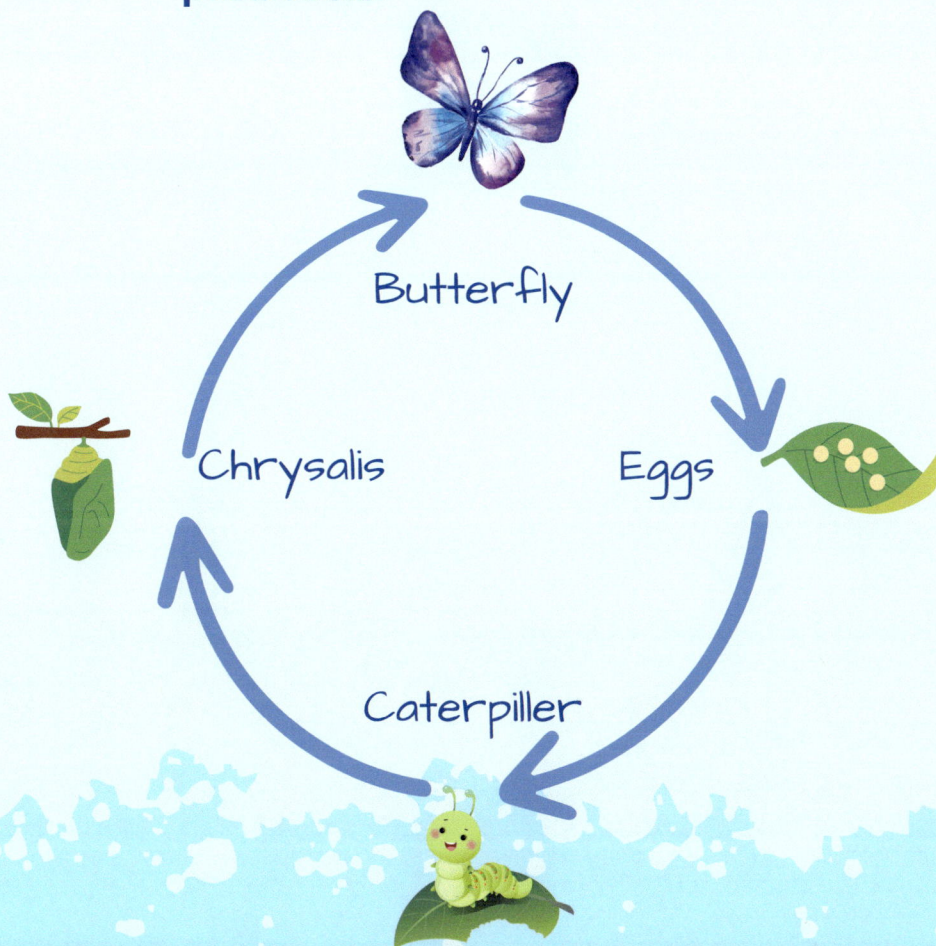

Butterfly

Chrysalis

Eggs

Caterpiller

Butterfly Field Notes

Keep notes of what you see!

Date	Time	Scientific Name	Common Name	Lifestage	Location

Butterfly Field Notes

Date	Time	Scientific Name	Common Name	Lifestage	Location

To Learn More!

BOOKS

🦋 **"Home is Calling - The Journey of the Monarch Butterfly" by Katherine Pryor (Author) & Ellie Peterson (Illustrator)**
A heartwarming story that follows the incredible migration of monarch butterflies. With vibrant illustrations and engaging storytelling, it's a perfect way for kids to learn about this amazing journey while fostering a love for nature!

🦋 **"The Life Cycles of Butterflies" by Judy Burris and Wayne Richards**
A wonderful, easy-to-follow guide with beautiful photos and clear explanations of butterfly life cycles. Great for curious young minds!

🦋 **"National Geographic Kids - Flutter Butterfly!" by Shelby Alinsky**
A National Geographic book designed for early readers, packed with fun facts and vibrant images of butterflies.

To Learn More!

WEBSITES

🦋 **The Butterfly Website**
A comprehensive resource for everything about butterflies—from identification tips to conservation news. There's also a fun "Butterfly FAQ" section for you to explore!

🦋 **Pollinator Partnership**
A comprehensive resource that focuses on protecting all pollinators, including butterflies. They provide educational resources and have initiatives like "Pollinator Week" that engage communities in conservation!

🦋 **Xerces Society for Invertebrate Conservation**
Dedicated to protecting insects, including butterflies, this site provides educational resources and information on how to create butterfly-friendly habitats in your backyard!

Glossary

Conservationist: A person who helps protect and take care of nature and wildlife.

Chrysalis: A hard, protective shell that a caterpillar makes around itself to stay safe while it transforms into a butterfly.

Crypsis: When an animal or plant hides or blends in with its surroundings to avoid being seen, like using camouflage!

Ecosystem: A big community made up of all the plants, animals, and their environment, like air, water, and soil, all working together.

Endangered: When an animal or plant is in danger of disappearing forever if we don't protect it.

Extinct: When there are no more of a certain species left anywhere in the world.

Habitat: The natural home where a plant or animal lives and grows.

Host Plant: A special plant that caterpillars or butterflies eat, or where they lay their eggs.

Iridescence: Colors that seem to change when you look at them from different angles, like a rainbow or a butterfly's wings.

Mandibles: The strong jaws that caterpillars use to munch on leaves.

Glossary

Metamorphosis: A multi-step process in which an animal changes as it grows up. For butterflies, it means changing from an egg to a caterpillar, then to a chrysalis, and finally into a butterfly.

Migrate: To move from one place to another depending on the season, like how some butterflies fly south for the winter.

Mimicry: When one animal looks like another to trick predators. Some butterflies pretend to be poisonous by looking like harmful ones!

Overwinter: When an animal survives through the winter, even when it's cold outside.

Pollinator: An insect or animal that moves pollen from one flower to another, helping plants grow seeds.

Proboscis: A long, straw-like mouthpart that butterflies use to drink nectar and water.

We hope you enjoyed getting a *little* glimpse into
The World of Butterflies!

We're excited to share something special soon.

Scan here and send us a message **"Butterflies"** for
your chance to win the surprise!

Limited availability - act now!

36

Made in United States
Troutdale, OR
11/21/2024

25140669R00024